RSS

THE PRIDE OF NATION MISSION AND VISION

RSS

THE PRIDE OF NATION MISSION AND VISION

Ram Nivas Kumar

MA (English), MLISc., MJMC, Dip-in-OA

Edition
2024
Copyright

PREFACE

The RSS is a nationalistic voluntary organisation. It is the largest patriotic organisation in the world. It has its own mission and vision. It is the protector and saviour of the whole society. It serves the whole humanity.

Some of my friends including academicians and high intellectuals have been asking me to write a book on RSS for a long. It struck my mind and led me to the deep learning of the RSS. After having a vast study of the RSS and getting to know its working and objectives, it occurred to me that writing a book on RSS could be very useful for our youth and other nationals. Hence, I have attempted this book.

The objective of this book is to bring into light the mission and vision of RSS to all people across the globe.

The book is based on the different literature and documents of RSS. We have sought some help from "Bunch Of Thoughts" by Guruji M. S. Golwalkar. We have also consulted some other books on RSS for reference and acknowledgement.

The youth and all other nationals of the world are requested to go through the book at least for once so that they can catch the correct views of the RSS.

We have taken utmost care about the accuracy of the content and language of the book. However, inadvertent errors, if any, may please be brought to our notice. Comments and suggestions are most welcome.

Hope, this book will help you know the RSS full well and you would like to read it a lot.

—Ram Nivas Kumar

CONTENTS

1. Introduction
2. RSS and Indian Independence Movement
3. RSS : Mission and Vision
4. Founder of the RSS
5. The Sangh Methodology
6. Sangh March : Its Thrust Area
7. RSS on Jammu and Kashmir
8. About the Organisation

1

INTRODUCTION

RSS is the abbreviated form of Rashtriya Swayamsevak Sangh. It is a national volunteer organisation. It is completely a patriotic organisation. It is widely regarded as one of the principal organisations of the Sangh parivar. It has its own commitment of selfless service to the nation. It is the world's largest voluntary organisation.

The initial impetus was to build up character through discipline and to unite the Hindu community to form a Hindu Rashtra (Hindu Nation). The organisation promotes the ideals of upholding Indian culture. It promotes the values of an ideal civil society. It propagates the ideology of Hindu culture to strengthen the majority of Hindu community. It drew initial inspiration from European right-wing groups during World War II. Gradually, RSS grew into a prominent Hindu nationalist organisation sprawling with several affiliated organisations that established numerous schools, charities, and clubs to spread its ideological beliefs.

RSS was founded on 27 September, 1925 by Dr. Keshav Baliram Hedgewar, a doctor in the city of Nagpur. He was a political and social activist. Dr. Hedgewar became a member of the Anusheelan Samiti, an anti-British revolutionary group, getting into its inner circle. Hedgewar organised anti- British activities through the Kranti Dal (Party of Revolution) and participated in Tilak's Home Rule Movement in 1918. According to the official RSS history, Dr. Hedgewar came to realize that revolutionary activities alone were not enough to overthrow the British. Being influenced by Sir Vinayak Damodar Savarkar, he founded RSS with the objective of strengthening the Hindu society.

Dr. Hedgewar believed that a handful of British were able to rule over the country of India because the Hindus were disunited; because the Hindus lacked vigour (parakram) and because the Hindus lacked a civic character. Therefore, he recruited energetic Hindu youth with revolutionary flavour. He gave them a uniform of black forage cap, khaki shirt (later white shirt, khaki shorts) emulating the British people and taught them paramilitary technique with lathi, sword, javelin and dagger. Hindu ceremonies and rituals played a large role in the organisation, not so much for religious observance but to provide awareness of India's glorious past and to bind the members in a religious communion. Hedgewar also held weekly session of what he called intellectual education consisting of simple questions to the novices concerning the Hindu nation and its history and heroes especially Shivaji. The saffron flag of Shivaji, the Bhagwa Dhwaj was used as the emblem for the new organisation. Its public task was involved in protecting Hindu pilgrims at festivals and confronting any resistance against Hindu processions.

After it passed two years in the life of organisation, Hedgewar organised an Officers Training Camp with the objective of preparing a corpse of key workers whom he called Pracharaks. He asked the volunteers to renounce their professions and family life and dedicate themselves to the need of the RSS. The tradition of renunciation gave the RSS the character of a Hindu "sect" that led to the development of Shakhas as possible first in Nagpur, then across Maharashtra and eventually in the rest of India. A Shakha at the Benaras (Varanasi) Hindu University was established. Other Universities were similarly targeted to recruit new followers among the students population. Three Pracharaks went to Punjab—Appaji Joshi to Sialkot, Moreshwar Munje to the DAV College in Rawalpindi and Raja Bhau Peturkar to the DAV College in Lahore in 1940. Madhavrao Muley was appointed as the Prant Pracharak (regional missionary) in Lahore. They all thought that there must be an organisation based on the country's traditions and history.

The initial meeting for the formation of the Sangh was held on the Vijaya Dashmi in 1925 between Dr. Hedgewar and four Hindu Mahasabha leaders—Balkrishna Shivram Moonje, Ganesh Savarkar, Laxman Vasudev Paranjpe and B. B. Tholkar. RSS took part as a volunteer force in organising the Hindu Mahasabha annual meeting in Akota in 1931. Moonje remained a patron of the RSS throughout his life. Both Moonje and Ganesh Savarkar worked to spread the RSS Shakhas in Maharashtra, Punjab and Delhi. Savarkar merged his own organisation "Hindu Sabha" with the RSS and had its expansion throughout the country.

2

RSS ANDINDIAN INDEPENDENCE MOVEMENT

RSS portrays itself as a social movement. After the formation of the RSS, Dr. Hedgewar kept the organisation free from having any direct affiliation with political organisation. In accordance with the Hedgewar's tradition of keeping the RSS away from the Indian independence movement, any political activity that could be construed as being anti-British was avoided. Hedgewar talked about Hindu organisation avoiding any direct comment on the Government. Hedgewar personally participated in the Satyagraha launched by Gandhiji in April, 1930. But he did not get the RSS involved in the movement. He sent information everywhere that the RSS would not participate in the Satyagraha. However, those wishing to participate individually were not prohibited. In 1934, Congress passed a resolution prohibiting its members from joining RSS and Hindu Mahasabha.

M. S. Golwalkar, who became the leader of the RSS in 1940, continued and further strengthened the isolation from the independence movement on his view. The RSS had pledged to achieve freedom through defending religion and culture and not by fighting the British. Golwalkar did not want to give the British an excuse for a ban on the RSS. He complied with all the structures imposed by the Government during the Second World War, even announcing the termination of the RSS military deportment. The British Government stated that the RSS was not all supporting any civil disobedience against them, and as such their political activities could be overlooked. The British home department took note of the fact that speakers at Sangh meetings urged its members to keep aloof from the anti-British movements of the Indian National Congress whose instructions was duly followed. The home department was thereby of the opinion that the RSS did not constitute a menace to the law and order in British India.

The Bombay government in a report appreciated the RSS that the Sangh had scrupulously kept itself within the law and refrained from taking part in the disturbances (Quit India Movement) that broke out in August 1942. It also reported that the RSS had not in any way infringed upon government orders and had always shown a willingness to comply with the law.

WORLD WAR II

During the World War II, RSS leaders openly admired Hitlar and Benito Musolini. M. S. Golwalkar, who became the supreme leader of the RSS, took inspiration from Adolf Hitlar's ideology of racial purity. RSS leaders were supportive of the Jewish State of Israel. Savarkar himself supported Israel during its formation. Golwalkar admired the Jewish to maintain its religion and culture.

PARTITION

The partition of India affected millions of Hindus, Muslims and Sikhs. They were attempting to escape the carnage that followed during partition. RSS then helped the refugee from West Punjab and other parts of the country. It also played a very active role in communal tolerance and shown examples of communal harmony.

3

RSS: MISSION AND VISION

For the welfare of entire mankind, Bharat must stand before the world as a self-confident, resurgent and mighty nation. At the very inception, the Sangh was viewed by its founder not as a sectorial activity but as a dynamic power-house energizing every field of national activity. The ideal of the Sangh is to carry the nation to the pinnacle of glory through organising the entire society.

THE MISSION

The Hindu culture is the life breath of Hindusthan. It is, therefore, clear that if Hindusthan is to be protected, we should first nourish the Hindu culture. If the Hindu culture perishes in Hindusthan itself, and if the Hindu society ceases to exist, it will hardly be appropriate to refer to the mere geographical entity that remains as Hindusthan. Mere geographical lumps do not make a nation. The entire society should be in such a vigilant and organised condition that no one should dare to cast an evil eye on any of our points of honour. It should be remembered that strength comes though organization. It is, therefore, the duty of every Hindu to do his best to consolidate the Hindu society. The Sangh is just taking out this supreme task. The present fate of the country cannot be changed unless lakhs of young men dedicate their entire life for that cause. To mould the minds of our youth towards that end is the supreme aim of the Sangh —Says Dr. Keshav Baliram Hedgewar, the founder of the RSS.

SANGH UNIQUE AND EVERGREEN

A unique phenomenon in the history of Bharat in the twentieth century is the birth and unceasing growth of Rashtriya Swayamsevak Sangh (RSS). The Sangh's sphere of influence has been spreading far and wide like the radiance of a diamond. Sangh inspired institutions and movements form a strong present in social, cultural, educational, developmental and other fields of nationalist endeavour. It has been increasingly recognized that the Sangh is a purely social and apolitical organisation with high nationalistic vision. It represents a corpus of thoughts and action firmly rooted in genuine nationalism and in the year old tradition of this country.

No other movement or institution has attracted such vast number of adherents as the Sangh has. Several thousands of adherents have made social work their life mission. Their character and integrity are not doubted even by their most virulent critics. As a movement for national restoration, Sangh has no match in Bharat or elsewhere.

Absence of idealism has been at the root of our most of the problems haunting our polity. Amidst such an environment, Sangh is unique in inculcation of patriotism in all citizens and in all life activities. Nation demands the fostering of seasonal character, uncompromising devotion to the Motherland, discipline, self-restrain and courage. To create and nurture the noble impulse is the most challenging task before the country—what Swami Vivekananda succinctly called man-making. It is to this historic mission that the Rashtriya Swayamsevak Sangh has addressed itself.

SANGHA DYNAMIC POWER HOUSE

Leaders of the Sangh anticipated the need for strengthening the foundation of the Hindu society and for preparing it for challenges on social, economic, cultural, religious, philosophical and political plans. A galaxy of servants such as Dayananda, Vivekananda, Aurobindo and Tilak had shown the seeds of the most recent phase of national renaissance. What was needed was a sufficiently strong instrumentalist for carrying process onward. This instrumentality was created and bequeathed to the nation by Hedgewar in the form of Rashtriya Swayamsevak Sangh which after years of deliberate and patient preparation founded in Nagpur on 27th September, Vijaya Dashmi day of 1925.

Erosion of the national integrity is in the name of secularism, economic and moral bankruptcy.Erosion of national integrity is in incessant conversion from the Hindu through money, power and even increasing trends of succession. Erosion of national integrity is through educational pattern dissonant with the native character of the people and state sponsored denigration of anything that goes against Hindu or Hindutva. These pervasive tendencies provide ample proof of the soundness of the foundation of the Sangh as conceived by Dr. Hedgewar and its continued relevance for the survival and health of the Hindu society and of the nation as a whole. It is the Rashtriya Swayamsevak Sangh alone which has consistently been sounding the alarm of all these wrong tendencies in the body-politic of Bharat.

Dr. Hedgewar often said, "Even if the British leave, unless the Hindus are organised as a powerful nation, where is the guarantee that we shall be able to protect our freedom!" His words have proved to be prophetic. Co-jointly with independence, parts of Punjab, Sindh and the frontier areas were sundered from Bharat. Even for seven decades of nation's efforts, Kashmir remains a thorn in the flesh. However, annihilation of Article 370 gave a bit satisfaction to the people of India.

Continuous efforts have been there to make Assam a state of particular majority. Some scrupulous persons are also trying to convert our Hindus. Even armed revolt has been engineered to carve out independent provinces. Such activities receive ready support and unlimited funds from foreign countries and agencies keenly interested in destabilising Bharat for their own ends.

Sangh's doing has been a genuine patriotic concern amid the cacophonous. Even at the inception, the Sangh was viewed by its founder not as a sectorial activist or movement, but as a dynamic power-house energizing every field of national activity.

A burning devotion to the Motherland, a feeling of fraternity among all citizens, intense awareness of a common national life derived from a common culture and our history and heritage- three- in brief- may be said to constitute the life spring of a nation. It is these sentiments which have to be instilled in each child. Obviously, this task is beyond the capabilities of political institutions. This is basically a social task. This is the mechanism Dr. Hedgewar evolved for fulfilment of all important tasks of the RSS. Dr. Hedgewar had the foresight to anticipate this need. He also had the skills of organisation needed to give a concrete shape to that concept.

4

FOUNDER OF THE RSS

Keshav Baliram Hedgewar was born on Varsha Pratipada, the Hindu New Year Day, on the 1st April, 1889 at Nagpur. Even as a child he stated questioning how a handful of foreigners could afford so long to rule over a vast and ancient nation like Bharat. No wonder that he threw away the sweets distributed on the occasion of the diamond jubilee of queen Victoria's coronation. He was eight years old at the time when studying at high school. At his meagre age he started participating in nationalist activities. The intensity of his urge to free the motherland grew steadily in 1908 when he was expelled from school for leading the students in raising the seditious cry of "Vande Matram." He had to move to Pune to complete his matriculation.

Hedgewar opted for a medical course in Calcutta chiefly prompted by the prospect of getting first hand acquaintances with the underground movement. He soon became a core member of one of the leading revolutionary groups called Anusheelan Samiti and also indulged himself into various social service activities. When the river Damodar was in floods in 1913, he rushed to join the relief team.

He returned to Nagpur in 1916 as a qualified doctor. However, he never intended to practice medicine despite dire poverty at home. Remaining a bachelor, he preferred to become a physician to cure the ills of the nation. By then, he had established active contact with stalwarts like Lokmanya Tilak, Dr. Moonje and Loknayak M. S. Arrat. He worked in responsible position in the Congress and Hindu Mahasabha till the early 1920.

Hedgewar's speeches of those days were sheer fire. It was not long before he had to face court trials. In one such trial, he defended himself declaring- "The Europeans and those who call themselves the government of this country should recognise that the time for their graceful exist is approaching." He was awarded one year rigorous imprisonment.

After release from prison, Dr. Hedgewar intensified his quest for an understanding of the true nature of our nation for whose freedom struggle was being carried on.

Bharat is not a nation born recently. It has been a nation for millennia. It had made phenomenal progress in science, commerce, arts, technology, agriculture and other spheres. Not to mention philosophy and the spiritual domain wherein its achievements continue to elicit wonderment to this day. It is also a fact of history that the cultural empire of Bharat extended to the whole of South-Asia for over four centuries. Equally, it is a sad fact of history that social disunity and dissension have been the cause of Bharat's political subjugation by alien invaders.

Dr. Hedgewar's response to this challenge was the founding of the Rashtriya Swayamsevak Sangh in 1925. The aptitude of one great mind can be fully grasped only by minds with a vision and imagination. Thus, even in the early days of the Sangh, it drew praise and approval from eminent stalwarts including Mahatma Gandhi, Savarkar, Subhas Chandra Bose, Madan Mohan Malaviya and others.

The first Shakha of the Sangh was started with a handful of youth at Nagpur. Gradually, Shakhas sprouted in other provinces. Soon there were a vast number of Pracharaks (whole time social workers) totally dedicated to nation building activities working for fulfilment of the Sangh mission. Dr. Hedgewar toiled day and night to lay a strong foundation for the growth of the Sangh.

From 1940 onwards, the task of steering the organisation as the second Sar-Sanghchalak came upon the shoulders of Sri Guruji (Madhav Sadashiv Golwalkar— 19.2.1906 - 5.6.1973). He made his tireless movement all through the year in each and every province meeting the Swayamsevaks. He inspired them to put in more time and energy. He made the Sangh grow rapidly even up to far off plague areas in Assam and Kerala. The Sangh which previously had only a few Shakhas in and around Nagpur, Vidarbha, Maharashtra and in some distant places like Lahore, Dehli, Varanasi, Calicut and Madras began to spread with its inspiring personality, far and wide, in the highly surcharged previewing political atmosphere of the country. Then, struggling for its freedom, with ever increasing number of Pracharaks submitting themselves for the Sangh, gave a further Philip to the process. Sri Guruji with his great erudition cogently propounded the historical and sociological background and concept of Hindu Rashtra which until then was just an empirical thought. He widened the ideological base of the Sangh asking to join the intelligible villagers and the urban intellectuals. Through his uncompromising stress on the one hour Shakha technique and through his own work and ideal, he perfected the Sangh methodology. As more and more co-workers imbued with ideology and organisational skill joined, the organisations like ABVP, BMS, BJS, BKVA, etc. began to branch forth as the circumstances demanded.

After the assassination of Gandhiji, the Sangh also had to go though unjust order of a ban, but ultimately it came out totally unblemished and as out of eclipse again continued with its mission. In 1973, after thirty-three years of service and unstinted stewardship, when Sri Guruji passed away, the responsibility was passed on to Sri Balasaheb Deoras (Madhukar Dattatraya Deoras (11.12.1915 to 17.06.1996), the third Sar-Sanghchalak. In his tenure of twenty years, the growth of the Sangh, apart from geographical spread far and wide, has been meteoric with leaping numbers of varied service projects and ever expanding horizons of the Sangh inspired organisation.

Balasaheb Deoras passed on the beacon of Sar-Sanghchalak to Prof. Rajendra Singh in 1994. He, in turn, delegated his responsibility to K. S. Sudarshan in the year 2000. In 2009, Sudarshan passed on his responsibility of Sar-Sanghchalak to Dr. Mohanrao Bhagwat under whose leadership the RSS is marching ahead on its way to accomplish its mission and translate the vision of a united, strong and prosperous Bharat.

5

THE SANGH METHODOLOGY

The ideal of the Sangh is to carry the nation to the pinnacle of glory through organising the entire society and ensuring protection of Hindu Dharma. To achieve this goal, the Sangh created a method of working in consonance with that ideal. Decades of functioning has confirmed that this is the most effective way of organising the society. The Sangh's method of working is of the simplest kind. The Sangh has always grown by personal contact. Coming together every day for an hour is the heart of the technique. This is a self-constrained mechanism. Hence, it is a success.

The daily Shakha is undoubtedly the most visible symbol of the Rashtriya Swayamsevak Sangh. The Shakha is as simple in its structure as it is grand in conception. No better example can be given to prove the truth of the adage that it takes a genius to simplicity or mechanical tool. After more than nine decades since the inception of the Sangh, people continue to express puzzlement as to how such a simple tool as the daily Shakha can produce idealists and patriots of such sterling worth, willing to dedicate all their energies and talents to the cause of the Motherland; willing even to bestow their lives, if need be to protect the honour of the Motherland. Herein lie the extraordinary vision, skill and foresight of Dr. Hedgewar, the founder of the Sangh.

WHAT IS SHAKHA?

A saffron flag called the Bhagwa Dhwaj flutters in the midst of an open playground. Youth and boys of all ages engage in varieties of indigenous groups. Uninhibited joys fill the air. There are exercises, *Suryanamaskar* and sometimes training in skilful yielding of *dandas*. All activities are solely disciplined. The physical fitness programmes are followed by groups singing patriotic songs. Also, forming part of the routine is exposition and discussion of national events and problems. The day activities culminates in the participants assembling in orderly rows in front of the flag at a single whistle of the group leader and reverentially reciting the prayer: Namaste, Vatsale Matrubhoome (My salutation to you, loving Motherland!). The prayer verses are in Sanskrit. Even as the group leader's various commands are all in Sanskrit. The prayer includes a heart-felt utterance of the inspiring incarnation—Bharatmata ki Jay.

There is the outline in the Shakha of RSS. The Shakha is the most attentive and time tested instrument for the moulding of men on patriotic lines—outreaching by far its physical dimension. The Shakha process is further strengthened by graded training camps called "Sangh Shiksha Varga" at provincial and all Bharat level at regular intervals.

The Sangh has popularised the observance of six national festivals of social significance—Varsha Pratiprda or Hindu New Year, Hindu Samrajya (Hindotsava) on Jyestha Shukla Trayodashi commemorating the coronation of Chhatrapati Shivaji, Gurupoojan on Asaadh Poornima, Raksha Bandhan on Shravan Poornima, Vijayadashmi on Ashwin Shuddha Dashami, and Makara Sankranti.

RIGHT WING POLITICS

RSS believes in right wing politics. Right wing politics holds that certain social orders and hierarchies are inevitable. They are normal, desirable and typically supportive. This position is on the basis of natural law, economics and tradition. Hierarchy and inequality may be viewed as natural results of traditions, social differences and the competition in market economy.

DEFINITION OF HINDUTVA

Hindutva (Hinduness) is a term popularised by Vinayak Damodar Savarkar in 1923. It is the pre-dominant form of Hindu nationalism in India. The Bhartiya Janata Party (BJP) adopted it as its official ideology in 1989. The notion of Hindutva (Hinduness) was coined in the early 20th century referring to the meaning of the Hindu, viz. Indian, the follower of Indian religions in general and follower of Hinduism in particular. Vinayak Damodar Savarkar, an Indian independence activist, disassociated the term Hindu from Hinduism. His title Hindutva defines a Hindu as one who is born of Hindu parents and regenerated

India as his motherland as well as holy land. The three essentials of Hindu are said to be the common nation (Rashtra), common race (Jati) and common culture (Sanskriti). Hindus are thus defined as a nation that had existed since antiquity.

A SEA CHANGE IN HINDU PSYCHE

People express doubt about the continued survival or growth of the Rashtriya Swayamsevak Sangh. However, such doubts after nine decades gave place to amazement as it has been the phenomenal growth of the Sangh. Today, there is not a single man or a single field of life which has remained beyond the purview of the Sangh Swayamsevaks.

This does not imply that it has always been smooth sailing of the Sangh. It has had to pass through many adversities. It was twice banned by the government, once in 1948 and again in 1975. And each time, the Sangh came out with redoubtable splendour.

The Sangh has survived and grown into huge dimension. The dynamism and vibrancy of the Sangh is the biggest and the most widespread movement of this kind perhaps in the entire world. A far truer index of the success of the Sangh is the greatly enhanced self-confidence now visible in the Hindu society. This is clearly evidenced by the warm public response which has greeted the hundreds of service projects. Gone are the days when Hindu society could be denigrated by all and sundry. Gone, too, are the days when reaping contempt on Hindu society by one or another was common.

The educational system initiated by Macaulay with the motive of producing an army of 'Brown-skin Englishmen to serve the imperial administration as the most obedient servants" was another legacy of the British rule in Bharat.

After independence, there was the direct need to reshape the entire system. In 1952, the first Saraswati Shishu Mandir, (nursery school) was founded in Gorakhpur, Uttar Pradesh as an attempt towards inculcating mandatory academic knowledge, discipline, patriotic outlook, love for motherland and high moral values. The attempt of Saraswati Shishu

Mandir is to inculcate Hindu principles, the thrust of education based upon a holistic approach to the physical, intellectual, moral and spiritual growth of the pupil. The small sapling of this Shishu Mandir has now grown into a mighty banyan tree as "Vidya Bharati", an umbrella body for thousands of educational institutions rising from nursery to post graduation level. The system of education being evolved by Vidya Bharati is based on age old Hindu values but having an outer structure in consonance with present day needs of modern education.

The systematic alienation of the tribal inhabiting remote forest areas form an inseparable part of the Hindu society through proselytization was another grave challenge that demanded immediate corrective measure. They are, though deprived of literacy, committed to their own rustic cultural moorings. They are also very talented. They had all along been the most exploited lot. They fall prey to unscrupulous conversion by Christian missionaries. It is to count this twin menace of British legacy that the Bharatiya Vanvasi Kalyan Ashram (BVKA) was founded in early fifties. The BVKA, now spreading over more than a hundred districts in 21 states, has been striving for the all-round development of the Vanavasis in their own natural surroundings enabling all their potentialities and talents to blossom.

While the Sangh was effective in organising the Hindus and inculcating in them healthy *"Samskara"* like discipline and social consciousness, the need for Vishva Hindu Parishad began to feel in the sixties for augmenting certain grey areas. For example, there was need to organise in about 150 countries and provide them with necessary arrangements for upholding their Hindu *Samskars* and faith in their daily lives. There was also need to bring all Sadhus/Sannayasis and orthodox Mathadhipatis on a common platform so that their combined influence could be channelized for the common good of the entire Hindu society. A mechanism to convert all those who had been knowingly proselytised to different faiths and are now desirous of coming back to the Hindu fold was needed. The VHP was founded in 1964 to fulfil this need.

With the end of the British Raj, Bharat became a democratic republic with a constitution of its own. Then, the need for a strong political alternative to the ruling party with unalloyed nationalism arose.

The Sangh, though preferred to remain apolitical, was well aware of its commitment to social transformation including political field based on Hindu values. In fact, politics was and has been wielding all-pervading influence over each and every field of social life, and as such there was need to evolve a totally new political culture in the country. It was in that contest that a few senior Sangh functionaries driven with the uncompromising commitment to Hindu nationalism decided to form Bhartiya Jana Sangh in 1951 under the presidentship of Dr. Shyama Prasad Mukherjee. The party, apart from electoral battles, had been waging for upholding the nation's integrity and honour. It was in the forefront of the "Save Kashmiri" movement in 1952.

6

SANGH MARCH: ITS THRUST AREA

The Sangh has often been misrepresented by its detractors—political or ideological, as having political motives or as a paramilitary organisation. The nine decade long growth of the Sangh and its ever growing influence over the society are sometimes attempted to be evaluated in political terms. But the Sangh, it must be remembered, is for attaining the "Sarvangeen Unnati" (all round development) of Bharat. And for this end, only the Swayamsevaks pledge to dedicate themselves. They do desire that the political field needs to be cleansed and reformed based on Hindu values and ethos. But politics is just one among the many facets of social life.

The Sangh has to its credit a few thousands of service projects covering various fields of social life. Apart from the projects, the Swayamsevaks are rendering services to the society individually and collectively wherever needed, whatever the cause. In fact, a Sarvodaya leader in appreciation of the services rendered by the Swayamsevaks to the cyclone hit victims in Andhra Pradesh in 1977 meaningfully said that RSS stood for "Ready for selfless Service." Obviously, the real purpose of the RSS is rightly understood by unbiased and discerning only.

The thrust of all *Samskar* in the Shakhas, though outwardly appears to be military like discipline, which in any case is essential for any nation building, is for imbibing the noblest qualities of head and heart. Admittedly, a Swayamsevak attending a Shakha is a common man with exposure to unhealthy and corrupt practices. In the Shakha, he, becomes broadminded and service oriented really to serve the society. In the Shakha, because of his interaction with the other members of society, his angularity becomes rounded off. The taste and the outlook get moulded for a purer plan where in place of self-aggrandizement the dedication for the services of the society becomes his fervent preoccupation with his *Samskar* rooted deep in his mind. Now, he considers participating in daily Shakhas a must as his routine work for that alone provides him the driving force for all his social work. He gets great satisfaction in applying all his energies for the amelioration of social maladies.

The Shakha, in fact, is not an end in itself. It is just a means to achieve the end. The programmes in the Shakhas are so structured that they develop a proper insight and make one aware of the deficiencies and drawbacks in the society. It also instils a sense of pride and intense love for its glorious cultural heritage and simultaneously awakens his commitment to work for his emancipation.

These men through the instrumentality of the Shakha are moulded. They enter various social fields to ennoble them with Hindu favour. Just as the pure blood flows out of the heart to reach each and every body cell taking along with it oxygen and nourishment; making it function properly and then returning to the heart to get itself once more energised, the Swayamsevaks also imbibe proper *Samskars* in the Shakha, and these propel themselves into diverse social activities.

The aim of the Shakha is to organise the entire Hindu society and not just to have a Hindu organisation within the ambit of this society.

Though started as an institution, the aim of the Sangh is to expand so extensively that each and every individual and traditional social institution like family, caste, profession, educational and religious institutions, etc. are all to be ultimately engulfed into its system. The goal before the Sangh is to have an organised Hindu society in which Dalits constitute and the institutions function in harmony and co-ordination. While this is easily perceived at the conceptual level, the institutional outer form of the Sangh is also necessary for internalisation of this habit of organised living but without making it a creed.

The Swayamsevaks consider the Hindu family as Janata Janardana—god incarnate. Any service rendered to human society by the RSS expects nothing in return. It is for them the worship of their god, the Samaj Roopee Parameshwar (God in the form of the society). The abject poverty, illiteracy, caste barriers, sense of high and low, untouchability, exploitation, lack of medical facilities etc. are to name just a few social maladies which call for immediate corrective steps. The prime concern of the Swayamsevaks in the country is now for such service activities. At the Shakha level, a soft orientation is now given for this purpose.

It is but natural that in a self-oblivious society like ours, the innate oneness and the fraternal bonds are the first cause. As such, the poor, the illiterate and the weaker sections in the society become an easy prey for exploitation and conversion to other faiths. The unsympathetic rich try to shake the blood of the poor and the crafty intelligent exploit the gullible. So apart from rendering positive service, the Swayamsevaks consider it equally important to combat such injustices on behalf of the weaker sections.

The Bharatiya Vanvasi kalyan Ashram, the Grahak Panchayat, the BKS, (Bharatiya Kisan Sangh) are all spearheading such movements for social justice whenever the need arises.

In a society divided on caste, class and language lines, the greatest service from a social worker to his community will be to keep intact the very social fabric, the oneness of the society being an article of faith with the Swayamsevak. It becomes all the more important for him to service for social consolidation, especially when the self- seeking politicians try to drive a wedge between diverse groups for their own selfish ends, and anti social elements take advantage of such sensitive situations. The unifying Hindu appeal generated by Sangh has always acted as a powerful ante-dote to the disintegrating pulls exercised by separatist element. In many a trying situation of conflicts born out of casteism, untou- chability and sectarianism, the Rashtriya Samarasta Manch at Maharastra, the Speak Sanskrit Movement of Karnataka and the like have been rendering yeoman service in this direction.

While founding the Sangh, Dr. Hedgewar, himself a freedom fighter, had before him the goal not only of independence but also of "swatantrya" in its literal sense, i.e. the blossoming of 'swa'- the national identity—in every walk of our social life. As such, it has always been the supreme concern of the Swayamsevak to uphold and seek re-assertion of the national honour wherever it is at stake.

7

RSS ON JAMMU AND KASHMIR

The state of Jammu and Kashmir has been a headache for our country since independence. The forces inimical to Bharat never wanted Kashmir to integrate itself with Bharat. And in October 1947, immediately after independence when Pakistani forces invaded Kashmir, evil elements conspired with the enemy to defeat every move to shun the situation from our side. However, thanks to the entire collaboration of the Sangh forces, then present at Jammu with the armed forces of Bharat, that Kashmir was saved. Had it not been for the premature and insensible cease-fire declared unilaterally by our own government, the chunk of our territory still under the siege of the enemy, our armed forces would then have driven out the enemy completely beyond the border and thus would not have been this problem of Pakistan occupied Kashmir (POK) which even now continues to be a scourge undermining the sovereignty of Bharat.

The problem of Kashmir, in fact, is one of our own making. Keeping in mind its unique demographic character, it has been enforced special status under Article 370 of the Constitution even after its total accession with Bharat. In 1952, Bhartiya Jana Sangh and Praja Parishad—those days the political front of the Sangh in Jammu and Kashmir State—jointly agitated against this special status and the BJS had to pay a heavy price in the death of Dr. Shyama Prasad Mukherjee, the founder-President of the Party in Srinagar.

Apart from the Kashmir issue, the Sangh has all long been in the forefront in each and every national campaign—be it "Ban Cow Slaughter" campaign of 1952, or the "Mass Collection Drive" for the Vivekananda Rock Memorial of Kanyakumari in 1963, or the later issue of "Ramajanambhoomi Temple", the Sangh Parivar has irrefutably established that the Hindu society would respond like a Virat Purush. The aim is to activate the dormant Hindu society to make it come out of its self-oblivion and to instil in it firm determination to set it right, and to make it to reassert its honour and self-respect so that no power on earth dares challenge it in the days to come.

TOWARDS THE HINDU CENTURY

Not only the context of Bharat, but also the globalisation re-confirms the validity of the foundation of RSS that the 21st century would be dominated by Hindutva and what it stands for is a prophecy which has been heard from many quarters including eminent historians. The need is to recreate the self-confidence of the people of Bharat.

8

ABOUT THLE ORGANISATION

Inspired by the great acts of service to humanity by social reformers like Swami Vivekananda, different state units of Seva Bharati were carried out for the welfare of economically weaker sections of the society all over the country since 1985. Rashtriya Seva Bharati is guided by the social service ideology of Rashtriya Swayamsevak Sangh. The Akhil Bhartiya Sadhu Seva Pramukh of RSS guides the organisation. It also represents the Akhil Bhartiya Pratinidhi Sabha, the highest decision making body of the Sangh Parivar.

RSS works on the principle like this: "Take up one idea—make that one idea your life- think of it; dream of it. And live on that idea. Let the brain, muscles, nerves, every part of your body be full of that idea. This is the way to success" —Says Swami Vivekananda.

WOMEN EMPOWERMENT

Rashtriya Seva Bharati has a large number of affiliated Seva Sansthans that provide vocational training to economically underprivileged women. It trains women in making handicrafts and decorative items and helps them to market these products.

Dr. Hedgewar was heartedly influenced by the writing of the Hindu nationalist ideologue Vinayak Damodar Savarkar and adopted much of his rhetoric concerning the need for the creation of a Hindu nation. Hedgewar formed the RSS as a disciplined centre consisting mostly of upper-caste Brahmins who were dedicated to independence and the protection of Hindu political, cultural, and religious interest. It (RSS) advocates for Hindu nationalistic agenda under the banner of Hindutva. The group is structured hierarchically under the guidance of a national leader while regional leaders are charged with overseeing the local branches. A major emphasis is placed on dedication and discipline- both mental and physical as a means to restore strength, valour, and courage in Hindu youth and the fraternity among Hindus of all castes and classes. Paramilitary training and daily exercises and drills are a part of this discipline. The RSS reveres Hanumana (in Hindu methodology, the commander of the monkey army. The RSS has historically played a major role in the Hindu nationalist movement on several occasions.

HINDU FUNDAMENTALISM

Hindu fundamentalism in India has been influenced more by nationalist than by religion because Hinduism does not have a specific sacred text to which conformity can be demanded. Hinduism is above all a symbol of national identity rather than a set of rules to be obeyed.

The nationalistic orientation of the BJP is reflected in its name which means the "Party of the Indian People." Similarly, the name of the Rashtriya Swayam sevak Sangh (RSS), a self-defence force, means National Volunteer Corpse. The RSS advocates the creation of a Hindu State. The principal concern of the group is the danger posed for the Hindu nation. The Scheduled Castes (formerly untouchables/so-called Harijans) and the lower caste Hindus—both groups have also vehemently opposed the proselytization in India. The nationalism of the BJP and the RSS is also reflected in the religious and moral demands in this respect.

9

BUNCH OF THOUGHTS: AT A GLANCE

"Bunch of Thoughts" is a great book. It has high nationalistic views. The whole book is subdued by patriotic vision. It has been written by Guruji Sri M. S. Golwalkar published in 1966. In this book, Golwalkar hails the glory of India and of Hinduism. He also excoriates those Indians who are not Hindus. He claims that the hostile elements within the country pose a far greater menace to national security than aggressors from outside.

A long chapter in the book challenges the patriotism of some anti-national groups. The book talks of their future aggressive designs against our country. In "Bunch of Thoughts", Golwalkar criticises democracy saying— "Democracy is to a very large extent only a myth in practice. The high sounding individual freedom only meant the freedom of a talented few to exploit the rest."

VIEWS OF THE RSS

RSS teaches loyalty and devotion to the nation. It teaches loyalty and devotion to the society and to the motherland. The unity and solidarity of motherland is taught to claim the highest sacrificial devotion. Everyone should enter into this spirit of devotion to the nation on the spiritual unity of land. All people are Indians or Hindus in essence. The mental commitment should be final and supreme.

The Rashtriya Swayamsevak Sangh is not merely a school for teaching ideas and ideals. It is a school for practical education in character building. The volunteers are trained in a series of camps. People participate for common discussion on history and national ideals and heroes. People take part in drills and physical exercises. They develop their habits and motives for services of the motherland.

Day meetings of Swayamsevaks in Shakhas are held. Bigger gatherings on the occasions of national festivals and the celebrations of the Days of heroes are made. Lectures and demonstrations are given. Attempts are made to inculcate courage, discipline, sense of service to society, respect for elders and the learned. This is a unique system of training to the young mind in the land called Bharat. This all happens in full consonance with the proud ideals and practices of Indian culture.

No whisper of hatred is heard in the camp or during routine activities of the volunteers. The positive image of the mother country is made to occupy the entire mind and heart of the Swayamsevaks.

The Hindus, Muslims, the Christians, the Jews and all other followers have perfect Upasana Swatantra and freedom of worship so long as they do not seek to destroy or undermine the national security. This should subordinate their exclusive claim for final and sole revelation vis-a-vis the national security. They could witness their faith in life and speech but they should not indulge in any unfair and unspiritual modes of conversion.

THE OBJECTIVE

The objective of the RSS is based on a philosophy of national culture. It envisages the whole of the nation. The outlook it offers has room for all minorities on condition of their whole hearted submission to the supreme value of the nation. The RSS says that the nation is a vehicle of universal truth. No entity is above the nation. There is no chauvinist nationalism of the kind associated with Mussolini and Hitler.

The national identity requires that the whole of national society including minorities should share in the best values of the past. They should appreciate national *dharma*. The national history should be re-written giving the truth without vanishes and all should appreciate the best values exemplified by the heroes of entire history.

Thus, these thoughts go on to delineate quietly and patiently the portrait of the best Indian society and pattern of values in all spheres of life in culture, philosophy and social order. Thus, the Sangh seeks to hold before us the mirror of the national mind.

THE SACRED TRUTH

It is clear that the mission of reorganising the Hindu people on the lines of their unique national genius, which the Sangh has taken up, is not only a great process of true national regeneration of Bharat but also the inevitable precondition to realize the dream of world unity and human welfare.

The fact is that the knowledge is in the custody of all of us. It is a divine thrust that when a person possesses a treasure of knowledge, he makes it available for the welfare of others. If he fails in that supreme duty, he ruins not only himself but also others. Hence, the sacred duty of preserving the Indian society in sound condition has developed upon us.

It is inevitable, therefore, that in order to be able to contribute our unique knowledge to mankind, in order to be able and strive for the unity and welfare of the world, we stand before the world as a self-confident, resurgent, and mighty nation. The RSS has resolved to fulfil this age-old national mission to unite the scattered elements of the Hindu society into an organised and invincible force both on the plane of the spirit and on the plane of material life.

10

CALL OF OUR NATIONAL SOUL
TRUE SPIRIT OF SERVICE

The supreme vision of God head in society is the very core of our concept of "nation."It has given rise to various concepts of our cultural heritage. This vision inspires us to look upon every individual of our society as a part of that Divine whole. All individuals are, therefore, equally sacred. Our service with discrimination among them is reprehensible. Thus, in our culture, the spirit of social service has been sublimated into worship of God.

There are millions of human beings all around us who live in hunger and destitution deprived of even the barest necessity of life, and whose stories of misery will move the stoniest of hearts. Once our life becomes soaked with this true spirit of service, we will feel that all our individual possessions, however abundant they may be, do not really belong to us.

They are only means of worship of God in the way of society. Our whole life will then be an offering in the service of society.

Upanishads say: "God permits all creation whatever is left over by Him. After offering Him, enjoy only that much. Do not rob what belongs to others."

Let us, therefore, acquire maximum of material wealth so that we can serve God in the form of society in the best possible manner. Out of all that wealth, only that minimum should be used for our sake, the denial of which will hamper our capacity for service to society. To claim for or make some more than that is verily an act of theft against society.

In the Bhagavad Gita, Narada says: "Take whatever is essential for bodily subsistence. To take more is an act of theft, and the person concerned deserves to be punished." Thus, we are only the truest society. Such a pure attitude of service will leave no scope for ego or self-adulation.

DUTY IN PLACE OF RIGHT

Today we hear the clamour for right everywhere. Our political parties, too, are rousing the ego in our people by constantly speaking of their right. Nowhere is heard any stress on duties and the spirit of selfless service. The spirit of co-operation which is the soul of society can hardly survive in a climate of asserting of egocentric rights. That is why we are finding conflicts in our national life today between the teacher and the taught; the labourer and the industrialist and so on. It is only by our cultural vision that the true spirit of co-operation and consciousness of duty can be revived in our national life.

SILENCE OR SECRET

We have to assimilate the eternal and life-giving essence of our culture. Obviously, this is a work of imparting cultural *Samskar* which is to take place in an atmosphere free from public fears. Silence is often mistaken for secrecy. Our culture does not advocate exhibition. For, the Hindu husband and wife do not display their love openly. The Hindu wife does not express her love through kisses, embraces, or screams. Our men do not indulge in exhibition but their face becomes aglow with love. And that love continues forever without fear of any break. Our culture has always taught us that restrain of emotion is more potent and charming than extravagant demonstration. As our way of expressing love is considered dignified, the silent method of working is also dignified.

11

TRUE NATIONAL GLORY

Our one supreme goal is to bring to light the all-round glory and greatness of our Hindu Rashtra. In order to have a correct grasp of this goal, we should understand what exactly this great glory "Param Vaishavam" as we call it in our Prarthana, connotes. Then, we have also to understand how to attain and maintain that glorious condition of our mission.

Ordinarily, the glory of a nation is measured in terms of its material affluence. There is no doubt that a national glory has essentially to be in affluence. All the necessities of life must be fully provided to every individual in the nation.

OUR VISION OF GLORY

Each nation has its own keynote in life and marches ahead in tune with its national ethos. Our Hindu nation has also preserved a unique characteristic since times immemorial. To us, the aspects of material happiness, i.e. *artha* (the amassing of wealth) and *karma* (the satisfaction of physical desire) are only a part of man's life. Our great ancestors declared that there are two more aspects of human endeavour— *dharma* and *moksha*. They built up our society on the basis of this four-fold achievement, the Chaturvidha Purushartha of *dharm, artha, Kama* and *moksha*. We are, therefore, called a highly moral, spiritual and philosophical people.

So when we think of the greatness and glory of our nation and of the necessity of the body, we not only think of its wealth and affluence;we not only think of all the means of satisfaction, but we also think of the mind of the individual which should be made to rise above all these things and place him in a position to which he is entitled as a human being. It is a matter of common experience that physical desires can never be satiated. The more one attempts to satisfy them, the more intense they grow even as fire blazes instead of going out when oil is poured into it. It is also well known that a person who has a bundle of unsatisfied desires can never be happy in spite of any amount of multiplication of the means for his satisfaction.

In foreign countries, for example, in spite of its boundless affluence and prosperity, the incidence of various sorts of heinous crimes and mental distress in all strata of society is growing at an alarming rate. Having kept in political and economic factors on the sole and supreme consideration in life, they have ignored the roots of spirituality which alone restrain and ennoble the human mind and nurture the human soul to grow and blossom in peace and happiness.

12

STRENGTH IS LIFE: WEAKNESS IS DEATH

The first think is invincible physical strength. We have to be strong so as none in the whole world may be able to overawe and subdue us. For that, we require strong and healthy bodies. The essence of our scriptural message is "Strength is life, Weakness is death." Swami Vivekananda used to say, "I want men with muscle of iron and nerves of steel." Body is the primary instrument for fulfilling our duties in life. Without an able body we cannot achieve anything. Even to see God, a healthy or strong body is required. God is not for the weak. Young men should, with proper exercises and healthy habits, develop strong bodies capable of resisting heat, hazards, exertion and undergoing the hardships of life with good cheers.

CHARACTER IS ALL

Physical strength is necessary. But character is more important. Strength without character will only make a brute of man. Purity of character of individual is the life breath of national glory and greatness. If endowed with character, we can achieve anything and without character we stand to lose everything. This is as true of nation as of individual. Therefore, the two aspects of character—individual and national are like the twine of the length of national glory.

13

COMMON SENSE FOR SUCCESS

Now suppose we have a strong body and a pure and devoted heart. But how to use the body and the mind! For that, we require intellectual acumen capable of grasping the realities and intricacies of the situations and deciding one's right conduct. We should, therefore, develop power of concentration and sharpen our intellect and acquire the power to pitch upon the right action on the right moment. And we should also be prompt and dynamic in acting upon the decisions.

Without such practical wisdom, all our goodness and strength will be of no avail. Many a page of disaster in our past history was a result of the want of robust common sense. Let us not forget that the path of national re-organisation is not a bed of roses. And without sagacity, mere sincerity will not avail us when faced with knaves and crooks. One need not be intellectual to achieve all skills and wisdom in the practical world. Even persons in the common strata of society can cultivate such wisdom. Each one of us should rouse within ourselves the conviction that I am born with living seeds of wisdom, which if properly nurtured, shall surely take me to success and strive to live accordingly.

FEARLESSNESS

Suppose we have a strong body, purity of character, a keen intellect, but no fortitude. What is the use? All the time circumstances are not going to favour us. We shall have to face obstacles and adversities. Fearlessness is the first virtue of a hero. It is the starting point of all other noble virtues. Even in the *Gita,* the enumeration of the various godly qualities starts with *abhyam* (fearlessness). Our founder, Dr. Hedgewar used to say that the work of national consolidation should proceed in such a way as it neither frightens anybody nor it will be afraid of anybody.

All our ideal heroes have been the embodiment of fearlessness and fortitude. The spirit of heroism is necessary even to worship God. A coward cannot do it. Nothing can be achieved by cowards either in this world or the other. If we are on the right path, there is no reason to be afraid of anything.

LOYALTY FIRST

We need first to have service loyalty to the nation. We should have an urge to develop this quality in ourselves. Only intense devotion to this ideal that we have placed before us will give us the necessary urge to equip ourselves with all the great qualities required for achieving the glory of our nation.

DUTY TO COUNTRY FIRST

There may be occasions when conflicts arise in our mind while fixing priority among our several duties. Then, we will have to discriminate among the duties. In such a situation, take a detached view and respond to the supreme call of the ideal that we have chosen for our life.

LIFE WITH AIM

The Hindu society is a living reality which we all feel and experience. Though we cannot define it, we must be able to appreciate the special features which mark out the Hindus as a destined people. We cannot say that merely because a particular individual is not a Muslim or a Christian, he is a Hindu by the process of elimination. In our country, the Hindu is often referred to by political leaders as non-Muslim. That is not a healthy and positive way of understanding our real nature.

To a Hindu, life is not without an aim. That aim is not of greatness measured in terms of power, position, name or fame. The realisation of his true nature- the innate spark of Divinity, the reality in him which does take man to the state of everlasting supreme bliss, is the one great aim before him. But man has only a short span of life.

SERVE PEOPLE

We are living in this world. We are surrounded by innumerable worldly charms and distractions. We must think over the real aim of life. We must think how to conduct ourselves so that we may be able to progressively realize during the course of our life. Man does not live alone. He shuns solitude. He is gregarious by nature. So, human beings came together and live as social beings in the form of society. Thus, he can live well. He can develop and manifest the best in him. He can thus rise in the social rung and progress towards the fulfilment of the aim of life. It means that the building up and maintenance of a social order capable of affording each individual full opportunities to identify himself with all the possessions is the best way for lighting up in the path of every individual towards the realisation of the ultimate truth. Service to humanity is verily service to God- this has been a special feature of our philosophy of life.

A Hindu is born to be trained in a life- long course of discipline and self-restraint which purify and strengthen him to reach the Supreme Grid in life. Let us not say that there are small things about which we need not worry. It is only such little things that go to discipline over life and give shape and strength in our character.

14

OUR GLORIOUS MOTHERLAND
THE GRAND VISION

The men born in the land of Bharat are more blessed than the gods themselves- so sing the gods. India is a land worshipped by all our seers and sages as *Matrubhoomi, Dharmabhoomi, Karmabhoomi* and *Punyabhoomi,* a veritable *Devabhoomi* and *Mokshabhoomi*. India is a land which has been, since hoary times, beloved or sacred Bharat Mata for us whose very name floods in our hearts with waves of pure and sublime devotion to her. This is the mother of us all- our glorious and sacred land.

MOTHERLAND

An ancient concept 'Bharat Mata' denotes that this is our mother. In our cultural tradition, the respectful way of calling a woman is by her child's name. To call a lady Mrs. So or the wife of Mr.So is the western way. We say: "She is Ram's mother." So also is the case with the name

"Bharat" for our motherland. It is up to us to keep allowed that highly evolved concept of divine motherland towards our land.

CHILDREN OF THE MOTHERLAND

Arya is an old and proud name, no doubt. But it has gone out of our history especially for the last thousand years. Moreover, the mischievous propaganda carried on by the British under the corner of historical research during the past centuries has struck deep into the minds of our people. "Bharatiya" too is an ancient name associated with us since hoary times. The name "Bharat" appears even in the Vedas. Our Puranas have also spoken of our motherland as Bharat and of our people as Bharatiya. In fact, it connotes the same meaning as Hindu. But today there is misconception regarding the word "Bharatiya". It is commonly used as a translation of the word "Indian" which includes all the various communities like the Muslim, Christian, Parasi etc. residing in this land. So, the word "Bharatiya" is likely to mislead us when we want to connote our particular society. The word Hindu alone connotes correctly and completely the meaning which we want to convey.

15

CALL FOR REAL DEVOTION

Hindu society, whole and integrated, should forever be the single point of devotion for all of us. The other consideration whether it is of caste, sect, language province or party should not be allowed to come in the way of that single minded devotion. That is the criteria for real devotion. We all rise and take the life-giving message as our innate unity to every Hindu heart.

What is integration? Integration is nothing less than propagating the spirit of identification with this true national stream, its tradition and its aspiration. National, communal and anti-national- all such words help nourishing and strengthening the national ethos and the "nation". All such groups who consider themselves distinct from this national ethos and act in opposition to the national interest and demand separate rights and privilege for themselves are to be called communal. If in any attempt to achieve their separate right, they attack the national society, whether it is the form of religious conversion or destruction or desecration of places of worship or insulting the memory of the great sons of this soil or in whatever manner, such groups should be termed "anti-national".

The Hindu in Bharat can never be termed "communal". He has ever been devoted to Bharat and ready to strive for its progress and uphold its honour. Values of Bharat are indeed derived from the life of Hindus. As such, he is the national hero and never communal.

COMMUNALISM

The expression "communalism of the majority" is totally wrong and misconceived. In a democracy, the opinion of the majority has to hold the swayin the day to day life of the people. As such, it will be proper to consider the practical conduct of the life of majority as the actual life of the national entity. From this point of view, effort to uplift the life of Hindu is national and not communal. The communalism is, thus, opposed to the spirit of democracy.

APPEASEMENT HARMFUL

It is detrimental to national life to adopt the policy of appeasement of such groups by meeting their anti-national demands. Indulging in bargaining with them for temporary ends could cause harm to national pride, honour, interest and beliefs. It would be great folly and travesty of truth to term right tendencies that oppose these perverted and national attitudes as communalism of Hindus. It is, in fact, the duty of every nationally conscious citizen to oppose such tendencies.

SEVEN TYPES OF COMMUNALISM

Communalism appears in several forms. The Hindu groups arraying of themselves against the Hindu people—in whose life stream the Bharatiya notion finds its true expression- are in a way communal.

These are second type of communalists in Hindu society itself who originally came into existence in the form of creeds as a manifestation of the many-sided Hindu genius but who later forgot the source of their inspiration and creation and began to consider themselves as being different from Hindu Samaj and dharma and who on that premise demand separate and exclusive political and economic privileges and achieve those demands and proclaim themselves to be different from Hindu society and take to various agitations. Buddhists and Sikhs are of this type.

The third type of communalism is of groups like Dravids Kazhagam and Dravida Munnetra Kazhagam who, on the fallacious assumptions of racial distinctness, claim separation, and who to achieve their ends spread hatred, enmity and violence against the trust of society.

The fourth type of communalists consists of those who rouse controversies in the name of touchability and untouchability. Brahmans and non-Brahmans face hatred and enmity. They have selfishness and demand for special privileges. This also creates communalism in our society.

There is the fifth type of communalism—the communalism of linguistic groups who indulge in spreading aversion, rivalry and hatred against other linguistic neighbours.

The sixth type of communalism is of narrow provincial feeling and of adopting unhealthy attitudes toward people from other provinces. South and North, Punjabi and non-Punjabi, a Marathi versus Kannada, Gujarati versus Marathi and Bengal-Bihar-Orissa differences are of this type.

There is the seventh type of communalism which aggravates differences amongst our people. Caste, creed, language etc. fan mutual hatred to achieve eternal ends. This is the most dangerous type of communalism rampant all over the country of which many political parties including the party in power are guilty. So long this the political type of communalism exists, it is well neigh impossible to eradicate any other form of communalism. If only this seventh type of communalism is eschewed, we shall find it less difficult to deal with the other forms of communalism. The more prominent types are pointed here. There may be some more; the minor ones.

ESCHEW OVER ATTACHMENT

Dharma is the eternal law of life which gives an arrangement for all times. It is all embracing. It is clear that within the fold of Dharma, particular forms of worship, based on wasted economic interests, may also exist over attachment to small creeds. Sub-beliefs create parochial feeling and become an instrument for spreading animosity and conflict in the path of achieving equality and harmony of economic and other secular interests. And hence, such over-attachment is undesirable.

THE WAYS AND MEANS

Regardless of caste or creed, every individual should be taught that it is the supreme duty of all the people of Bharat to proclaim unhesitatingly the truth of the Hindu Nationhood of Bharat and to make it strong, prosperous, virile and sovereign. Intense devotion to this Nation should be roused in one and all.

While respecting and protecting the religions of non-Hindus, arrangement should be made to impart *samskars* to them to love and respect for the tradition, history, life attitude, ideals and values of the nation.

NO DIVISIVE TALK

In secular life all citizens are equal. This principle should be strictly adhered to. We must try a complete halt to forming groups based on caste, creed, etc., and demanding exclusive rights and privileges in services, financial aids, admission in educational institutions and all such other fields. Talking in terms of parties and communities should be totally put to an end.

RIGHT LANGUAGE POLICY

A free nation has its own language. For mutual intercourse, out of several national languages, India has accepted Hindi as its official language from the point of view of cause and convenience. But in the name of making it a good practice in the whole country, we are playing regional appeasement. This attitude towards official language or to treat it at par with English should be discarded. The aim of Sangh is to establish the integrated feeling of oneness of the nation with the medium of communication as Hindi.

16

BASIC CONCEPTS BROADLY SPEAKING

The people whose loyalty to the country and her tradition, to her heroes, to her security and prosperity, down the centuries, is undivided and unadulterated are national.

People who think in terms of their sect, caste, language or so-called race in contradiction to the rest of the people are communal.

People who strive for their own limited benefit and who strive for enjoyment of political power are communal.

People who strive for enjoying special rights and privilege not claimed or employed by the general people who envy, oppose and sometimes take recourse and go to violent means are communal.

Group whose loyalty is divided and is under suspicion and, in case of conflict, who is indifferent to the interests of the country and choose to serve other objects of their faiths are hostile are communal.

Groups who continue to believe themselves to be aliens, aggressors, victors, and erstwhile masters and rulers of the country are aliens evidently. People who have desires to really establish themselves as rulers are also hostile.

Those who think nations would, out of some perverted notions, strive to break away from the people as a whole and form themselves into a separate and conflicting state are anti-national.

Those who would not hesitate to join hands with those mentioned as above to achieve their ends, or would like to or actually try to league with any foreign power for these ends are traitors.

Political parties who protest their ideology forming the basis of foreign powers are traitors. Political parties who prefer such power to the country are enemies.

Political parties who tolerate, justify, or overtly or covertly assist such powers even against our country are enemies.

Political parties who assist foreign powers in case of their aggression on our country are both traitors and enemies.

Unfortunately all such classes exist in our holy land, a proper and fearless understanding of which is essential to the building up of a strong and integrated national life. Traitorous individuals amongst the true nationals and patriotic individuals amongst the other groups may be found. Let us learn to discriminate between individual qualities and psychology of the masses. It is common experience that patriotic individuals in other groups are swept off when mass friendly burst forth.

17

WHEN NATIONALISM GOES COMMUNALISM COMES

Man does not live by bread alone. He

must have a faith to live by and differ with. Without such a faith, life loses its diction and meaning, and man begins to drift. Till the rise of science, Christianity provided the necessary faith for European life. But science made mincemeat of Christianity. It blasted the Christian concept of time, space, life and the world. It gained a new faith in science. Indeed, science became its new religion. Then, people believed science to be omniscient and omnipotent as is God thought of in any religion.

MEETING THE HISTORY

The founder of the organisation used to put forth the aim of the Sangh in a small pretty sentence, "We have to organise and make our Hindu society so powerful that no power on the earth can dare cast an evil upon it." We are duty bound and we musthave to do this.

What makes us say that we are duty bound is to devote ourselves to this mission of organising our society. Firstly, we are all sons brought up in this society. The happiness and security of our individual or family life have been made possible by the fact of our birth in our society. Ours is an Indian society which has given birth to the greatest personalities in all walks of life and has evolved the highest philosophy. The greatness of the sages can be seen even to this day when others refer to the son of this soil as the descendant of a Rama, a Krishna, and Shankaracharya."

GREATER IN ALL RESPECTS

We had a free and flourishing national life of our own Motherland. We had a unique social order and highly evolved political institutions. We have to resolve to eradicate that basic malady by making our mother society once again united, organised, vigilantes and resurgent with an intense spirit of national consciousness and cohesion. To that end, let us approach every son of this soil with the message of united nationhood bound with ties of mutual love and discipline.

BE HINDUS TO THE CORE

All perversions have to be nipped in the bud. The great qualities of head and heart have to be planted in the young minds right from the elementary school stage. This can be done only when we draw upon the limitless storehouse of our ancient as well as modern literature which depicts our sublime national ethos and our mighty national heroes and events. Especially, our young men must be made to feel proud of being born in the great lineage of Rishis and Yogis. If we have to live up to their legacy, we must live as Hindus. We must appear as Hindus and also we must make ourselves feel by the whole world as Hindus. It is only when we learn to respect ourselves, our national customs and manners that we can hope to command respect from the outside world also. In fact, the world wants us to be true to ourselves and not to become mere carbon copies of some A, B, C.

FORGET NOT THE BASE

Depth of love and wisdom can be touched only if we start giving the necessary training right now to our infants. The right type of atmosphere has to be created from the elementary school age itself. Without the firm base of nationalism, to speak of humanity and internationalism would be losing at both ends. And so far as our own national philosophy and heritage is concerned, it has always embraced within its fold the highest good of all humanity. As such, preaching of atavism even in its most intense form will never divert the minds of our children from the highest value of human welfare.

WHY FIGHT SHY TO SAY HINDU

The first thing that strikes our eyes is that many of our educated Hindu brethren feel shy, if call themselves Hindus. Some special arguments are advanced to support their voice that they need not call themselves Hindus.

Secondly, we find that our Hindu society has been broken into so many bits and fragments. The countless divisions of castes, sects, creeds, and languages present dismal picture of disintegration.

ONLY WAY OUT

The only way out is to be courageous enough to declare a unitary type of Government by suitably amending the Constitution. The court is one, the people are one. Therefore, let us have only a single Government; a single legislative Authority. The country may be arranged into various roles from the points of view of administrative convenience. The tone may be few or many. That does not matter. The executive authority may be distributed, but the legislative authority should be one. There are some who say that many provinces and provincial legislatures are necessary to satisfy the demands of democracy. I have not been able to understand what connection there is between democracy and having many Legislatures. One central legislature for the whole country should satisfy the demands of democracy.

However, the person at the helm of affairs seems unable to master courage to opt for the unitary state. Then, the present Federal structure has to continue. It is essential that definite principles must be formulated by all and they must be stuck to. If there are smaller units with languages as only one of the basic factors, that should be welcome. States with more than one language or the more states with one language may be formed keeping in view the overall national interests. Smaller units need not be always harmful. As a matter of fact, tiny states have been formed in the old province of Assam where it is positively doing. The British has kept the so-called NEFA separate from the rest of Assam. The same tradition is being carried forward by our Government also. Now NEFA has been given a different name so that its separate entity has been confirmed. Apart from that, a small state called Meghalaya and another Mizoram have been formed.

TRUTH IS TRUTH

Truth must be spoken and experienced. It must be lived up to. Unless we do this, real national integration as a whole cannot be realized. As a matter of fact, even some Muslims and Christians who are really well meaning and patriotic at heart and are not ridden by old dreams of their empires do accept that this has been Hindu land for thousands of years and its national ethos are the Hindus ethos. But unfortunately, such persons are very few and are not vocal.

RESPONSIBILITY IS OURS

If once we all are Hindu, whatever our political and other denominations, we decide to stand shoulder to shoulder in a concerted manner as one national entity right from the Himalayas to Kanyakumari and from Dwarka to Manipur. There are some others who have been in this country since long. They also learn to respect the motherland and the nation of this entity. Keeping their own faiths intact, these would be able to become useful members of the great nation.

Hence, the RSS has been emphasising that the revitalization of the truth of our national existence alone will be asked to inspire our people for united and dedicated efforts in the cause of the nation. That alone will make our nation march forward with high strength and confidence holding its head high amidst all the turmoil and conflicts surrounding us in the world.

18
THE POTENCY OF NATIONAL LIFE

WORLD OF REALITY

The children of this great and ancient nation naturally desire that our nation should call every new height of prosperity, glory and honour in this world. This is a very legitimate desire. No one can deny it. However, life is not all smooth sailing in this world of hard reality. Even in the fulfilment of just and legitimate desire, one is confronted with groups of human beings called nations.

THE GREAT FACT

The world, as it obtains today, is divided into groups of human beings called nations which are constantly competing with one another for greater power and prosperity and greater dominion over wider territories of the globe. This has been the unfailing feature of human history right from its beginning.

MIRAGE OF MUTUAL FRIENDSHIP

What is the way out to maintain our national integrity and glory in this world of conflicts? Can we depend upon the friendship and alliance of other nation? Friendship and hostility between any two nations have never been a permanent future. Nations change their friends and foes as it suits their self-interest. Today, the world appears to be divided into two power blocks. Seeing their power and splendour and our own weakness in comparison, there are some who advocate our joining the one or the other block so as to be able to breathe fully under protective wing.

The moral is too evident. The friendship between the strong and the weak is bound to rescue the strong taking away the profits and leaving the weak to suffer the losses. That is what we witness in the international frontier.

MORALITY FROM TOP DOWN

How to control self-interest from running amuck? Suppose we advise all people and give them lectures. Will Sadhachar Samitis and mass pledges in public achieve that miracle? Mere lectures on morality and pledge shall never correct people's moral. Further, many persons who lecture on morality and administer pledges are such as we should not look into their lives.

If the top men are morally upright, morality will trickle down to the best stratum of society. You cannot build the character from bottom to top. It has always to be built up at the top. On the other hand, physical comforts have to be provided from the bottom. Feed them who are at the lowest rung of the ladder of our social life; who are physically weak and labour hard day and night and leading an existence which is certainly an insult to the dignity of the society.

TO IMPART SAMSKARS

It is necessary that our Hindu brethren who have imbedded the right *samskars* should meet regularly with a view to kindling among all our people. It will not be enough if we congregate on certain occasions and for some special programmes only. Even in our Shastras, nritya (dance), geet (music) and vadya (instrument) are mentioned. But they were useful only if used with the definite purpose of imparting *samskars*. Mere music and dance by themselves do not constitute culture. If the entertainment aspect alone is taken up, our cultural value stands ignored. It would surely lead to social degeneration. If the awareness of reviving Hindu values is to be made intensely and continuously alive, regular assemblage with suitable *samskar* imparting programmes is a must. Apart from the regular assemblage, there should be daily singing of *bhajans* and *shlokas* at home. Especially, the children should be taught to recite the same with due devotion and earnestness. And where there are our temples, the Hindus should cultivate the habit of congregating on certain holy occasions and conduct programmes like *satsanga* and *havans*.

Keeping close contact with learned men and spiritual teachers who visit countries to start suitable programme would be great help in furthering the above mentioned objectives.

ASSIMILATE THE GOOD

It is said that our people who go abroad are carried away by the superficial attractions there and do not try to go deeper to find out the real good points in the life of those people. No people on the face of this earth are entirely without some abiding virtues, nor will they be endowed with all the necessary noble qualities. We should be able to discriminate and make a dispassionate assortment of their virtues and vices and so one of our own strong points and weak points. We shall then be able to achieve a harmonious blend of the elements, excellence in both the systems. Our intelligent young men who are staying abroad should take up such comparative study and enlighten our other brethren there with the result of their findings.

There are indeed very pious people worthy of emulation in all countries. We should do well to emulate their examples. There are so many inspiring items of their literature which we could make them our own. Many of our sublime thoughts are echoed in their poetry and philosophical works.

RESPOND TO LOCAL ASPIRATIONS

There is an important aspect of cultivating the right attitude and pattern of behaviour towards the local population. The first thing that our brothers abroad have to bear in mind is that while carrying on a profession, an employment, the earning and amassing money should not be sole aim. They should understand and appreciate problems of the local people and sympathise with their aspirations. Some portion of their earnings should be kept apart for promoting their welfare and enlightening them on the great principles and values of Hinduism. At the same time, they should, by their personal example and living, demonstrate that they are coming from the land of a great and hoary culture and thus set a personal example to others.

BE THE WORLD MISSIONARIES

In a nutshell, our brethren abroad will have to bring about a total transformation in their thoughts and life styles, if they have to lead a happier, richer and more honoured life abroad and also make an image of Bharat shining brighter in those countries. All in order to do this is that we as a great people charged with a world mission should be vibrant in our hearts. That, sacred duty and thrust are cast upon us for bringing home the entire humanity the sublime truths embedded in our dharma.

19

UNTOUCHABILITY : CURSE AND CURE

The malady of untouchability among the common mass of people is that it is a part of dharma, and it is transgressing to our beaming sin. This religious perversion is the chief reason why this pernicious practice has continued to strike to the popular mind till now in spite of dedicated efforts put in by a host of religious stalwarts and social reformers over centuries. Guru Nanak, Ramanujan, Shankardeva, Swami Dayananda, Gandhiji and Veer Savarkar to name them only a few have striven their utmost to eradicate this standing blot on Hindu society. But the blot remained. Even now, the so-called higher castes refuse to treat the so-called untouchables as their equals. This social evil draws sustenance from the religious misconception. The traditional *mathadhipatis* who are looked upon by the people at large the authentic spokesmen of dharma should come forward to this anti-religious practice. The entire Hindu society should be consolidated with the spirit of indivisible oneness and that there should be no disintegration in it because of tendencies or sentiments like touchability and untouchability. The Hindu all over the world should maintain the spirit of unity and equality in their mutual intercourse. It goes without saying that if anyone is suffering from any disability, social or political, on account of what is called caste, this must be removed completely. Dr. Ambedkar had envisaged the special privileges for "Scheduled Castes" for only 10 years from the day we became a republic in 1950. But it is going to be extended. Continued special privilege on the basis of caste only is bound to create a separate entity. That would harm their integration with the rest of the society.

There are persons who are in real bad circumstances in all sections of society. There is no caste which is without poverty. The needy and the destitute are in every caste. It would, therefore, be proper that privileges should be based on the economic conditions of the people that will ease out matters and give proper solution acceptable to all. That, the so-called Harijans alone who are enjoying privileges will also be removed.

20

RSS VISION FOR SUCCESS

In Sangh, there is no trace of any dissension on account of caste, sect or language or on any other score. Thousands of Swayamsevaks draw from all strata of society.They sit and eat together. They play and sing together. They all do together without so much knowing to what castes or sects others belong to. It is now up to us to go to these neglected brethren and strive our outmost to better their living condition. We will have to work out plans by which their primary needs and comforts could be satisfied. We will have to open schools, hostels and training camps to equip them to benefit from these schemes. Along with physical amelioration love and pride in Hindu dharma and the spirit of identity with the rest of Hindus have to be rekindled in their minds through the channel of devotion to God. For that, we have to give up false notions of high and low and mingle with those brethren in spirit of equality. We should freely mix with them; eat with them; and sing and chant with them the holy singing of devotion.

SANGH VIEW ON TRIBALS

There is a problem of wandering habits of the tribes. How can they be given any training or *samskars* when they do not stay at one place at all for any length of time? No doubt, the Government is trying to do something for them. But the Government is after all machinery. And machinery cannot change the behaviour pattern of people. It is the human touch that can make over tribal brethren to a settled life. We could domesticate even the wild animal roaming in the jungle. Can we not persuade our own people to take to better and more refined ways of life?

LESSONS FROM THE PAST

There is one point on which we have to be especially forward. And that is the census. Our previous experience shows that the followers of

Islam increased more rapidly in proportion to those of the Hindus. The Hindus should not remain ignorant of the potency of their numbers. They should all, without fail, register themselves with the census. Further, all Hindus, to whatever sect, caste, clan, or tribe they may belong, must put down their community as Hindu only. Our brethren in the far Eastern region—they may be Naga, khasi, Jayantia, Mikir, Mizo, etc.—all should designate their community as Hindu only whatever may the differences be in their ways of dress, language, food or local customs. The basic truth about our single society is always to be borne in mind.

RSS VIEW ON FOREST DWELLERS

When we go and mix with those forest dwelling brothers, we find that the people are with qualities such as courage, intellect, industry, honesty, warmth of their culture and spiritual attainment. They form some of the finest men of our armed forces. Probably, it was only Maharana Pratap who had established close links with them and made them equal partners with society. The forest dwellers in those regions—the Bhills stood shoulder to shoulder with Rajputs generations after generations in the heroic defence. It is wrong to say that our social system was at the root of their neglect in olden times. The panchayat system was the basic unit of society. The forest dwellers had an honoured life. We find it mentioned in the description of the political system as early as during the reign of Sri Rama.

RSS HAS THE VIEW TO SERVE ALL

Many workers appear to take a delight in blaming others for all ills. Some may put the blame on the political perversities, others on the oppressive action of the Christians or Muslims and such other faiths. Let our workers keep their minds free from such tendencies and work for our people and for our dharma in the right spirit. Let our workers lend a helping hand to all our brethren who need help and strive to relieve distress. In this service, no distinction should be made between man and man. We have to serve all, be he a Christian or a Muslim or a human being of any other persuasion. Calamities, distress or misfortunes make no such distinction but affect all alike. And in service to relieve the sufferings of men, let it not be a spirit of concession or mere compassion but a devoted worship of the land. Let us have the true spirit of our dharma of surrendering our all in the humble service of him who is Father, Mother, Brother, Friend and Everything to us all. And many of our actions succeed in bringing out the glory and effulgence of our *Sanatana-Eternal-Dharma*.

HOW HEARTLESS WE ARE!

There is a factor of human touch that we are falling short with. This shortcoming is to be found not only in factories but also in villages. It is in cities. It is in the everyday life of our entire people. For instance, in every province of our country, there are vast areas where our people are ill-fed, ill-clothed, illiterate and devoid of any opportunities to cultivate religious devotion. They are exploited by many ways. We should be aware and take care of all this.

Proper upkeep of temples should also be the special responsibility. People of local bodies should be established to look after the arrangements for daily worship for its cleanliness and sanctity. An overall trust can be formed later on to control and guide the affairs of the temples in the spirit for which the temples are built. The present state of neglect and dilapidation of many of our temples is a sad reflection on our callousness towards our gods and goddess. If the heart is large, funds and every other kind of resource will flow automatically. Surely, our Hindu society will rise once again with full prosperity and glory that will make every heart of the world generous and devoted.

CALL TO MOTHERLAND

Our mothers have a special responsibility of gearing up the budding generations of our society. The essential aspect is to inculcate in them the right type of *samskars* such as devotion to duty. They have to be mindful of the many little things which became improper fashion among the young minds.

RSS VIEW ABOUT DRESS FOR SAMSKAR

Then about the dress, it must be borne in mind that the dress and decorative items also have their imprints on the young minds. Mothers should know that the children acquire traits of our culture through these things also.

IMPRESS THE RIGHT VALUES

Further, let there be an impress of national pride in all that is ours. Make a vow of *swadeshi* in all the daily household uses that will make for unsullied national character. The Hindu was known for his unflinching devotion to truth. They set thrilling character. But these days, even our big leaders have become notorious for their corruption and moral decay. It is up to our mothers to save our younger generation from such corrosive influences. This should so cultivate the atmosphere in home as would mark one gladly prefer to forgo a meal rather to accept immoral gratification. The family as a whole should pledge themselves not to be a part of the sinful food procured by corruption. If our mothers were to inculcate such wholesome and heroic traits in their children, surely the coming generations could be able to successfully meet the various challenges being faced by our country.

IF SOCIAL COHESION IS LOST

There is the question of our attitude towards the society. It is clear that the security and happiness of personnel and family life depend very much upon the well being of the society. It becomes difficult to survive, if society disintegrates. As such is the duty of first importance for us to see that social life is made healthy. In the past, we ignored this aspect of keeping our social life intact with self-respecting. We forget that we have to shine as one integrated entity. Our tremendous power is succinct to the feeling of being alone.

DUTY TOWARDS NEIGHBOURHOOD

There is a special burden upon our mothers of serving our needy sisters in society. A majority of our mothers will not be in a position to go far off places to carry on social work among the distressed and the destitute. However, this does not mean that they should sit back in their homes all the while. They could establish useful contacts among the women folk in their own neighbourhood and carry out programmes which would inculcate our cherished ideas among them and their children. The spirit of mutual help and service would also have to be made popular through our day to day social intercourse. Our women folk should not be allowed to develop inferiority complex or a feeling of helplessness. They should be taught that they all are living emblem—a *parashakti*.

SERVICE TO THE NEEDY

We see scattered around us a number of our sisters who are either engaged in physical labour or are totally helpless and handicapped. When we see such a sigh, our hearts melt and well up with deep compassion and motherly affection. We have to check out suitable projects which would give them some useful employment and enable them to earn a livelihood. It is our sacred duty to see that none of our sisters and others will be left on the streets scared for.

Literary campaign among women is more important programme which our educated mothers alone can successfully tackle. Imparting *samskars* to our people should be given the priority; teaching of alphabets should come in the second. In order to do this, instil in them the spirit of pure devotion to our motherland. Instil in them the faith in our dharma and pride in our history. Show them the map of our sacred motherland, the holy streams and mountains. Show them the *tirthas* and temples stretching right from the Himalayas to Kanyakumari. Introduce them the rich variety of our national life in language, literature, and social tradition. These make them become intimate with the true spirit of our national being.

INVOKE THE SPIRIT OF SAVITA

If our mothers make a reason to uplift the society, then there is no power in this world which can defeat them. The ideal of Savitri before who even the Lord of Death accepted defeat is before them. They all invoke within themselves such single minded devotion to the ideal of purity of character and such fearless heroism! Once we do this, we are sure, the long night will pass and a new dawn will spread its golden hue over the horizon of not only Bharat but over the entire world with the renewed effulgence of our dharma. Gandhiji had foreseen for the future of our dharma. He said: "Hinduism is a relentless growth. It is because we are fatigued, and as soon as the fatigue is over, Hinduism will burst forth upon the world with brilliance perhaps unknown before."

WE AND OUR STUDENTS

It does not seem right to regard the students as community different from the rest of the society. They are the integral part of our society. It is our duty to upbring and educate them in a proper way with a nationalistic view. Our education is mere informative and not innovative. The emphasis on somehow equipping oneself to earn a living and not on drawn out the personality of the youth. The ideal of improving the standard of living requests only to material well being in multiplication of wants and means of satisfying the carnal and mental cravings of the animal in men. It does not relate to developing the mental, intellectual and the higher aspect of the human being. The natural result is the production of an inordinate desire for amassment of wealth. We need cultural activities. The expression "cultural activity" has come to denote singing, dancing and such other activities which easily rouse the basic instincts of man. Such qualities inculcate the correct sense of values and restraint upon one's emotions and impulses.

21

MAN MAKING EDUCATION

Suffice to say that the whole system of education needs a complete change. Every student must be taught the basic principles of dharma and the life history of great ancestors who lived and demonstrated their high principles. We must teach our students the correct and true history of our people with the strong national heritage. They must also be given some preliminary training in the science of mind-concentration through simple yogic exercises. The rest of the education has necessarily to relate to the surroundings. Our students should be well aware of the facts of day-to-day life. We should equip them to successfully face the trials and tribulations in life. From the very beginning, the emphasis that the duty is uppermost must be persistently given upon the minds of the young in their formative years.

THE IDEAL THAT INSPIRES

To achieve this end of inculcating a correct sense of duty, our system of education needs to be ideal oriented. The word 'ideal' is likely to give rise to differences. But we hope that all will agree to certain broad fundamentals. The human being is wayfarer on the path to the ultimate Supreme Reality. That reality can be attended by devoted and selfless service. It is through service to Man that we can serve the Reality. Service to man has to begin with service to the group with whom we have a natural bond of affinity of ancestry, heritage, tradition, national entity and grateful devotion to the holy motherland which fosters us all and common devotion to which unites us all in one National personality. These are our basic ideas or aspects of our common ideal. A firm grounding in dedication to this one ideal is calculated to induce community of will, of mental and intellectual co-ordination when coupled with this co-ordinate will. Co-ordinated and controlled physical activity makes what is known as discipline. Military training can produce co-ordinated action on the physical plane. It is good so far if it goes. And to a good extent, it is a necessary complement to education. From the impressionable school going age, military training needs to be imparted. It should be necessary for joining armed forces. Mere military training cannot by itself inculcate the real spirit of discipline unless concerted efforts are made to instil the discipline of will which is born out of common devotion to one great ideal.

THE RIGHT SURROUNDINGS

All amenities so granted in the educational institutions have to be directed towards this goal. The amenities available today are to be the nature of pleasure. These also have a place in student life. But the whole atmosphere needs to be changed with the spirit of learning, with the spirit of making one's contribution to knowledge and with the spirit of the pious ambition to making one's mark in the ideal service. I think that suitable extra-curriculum activities have to be provided in the form of sports and physical exercises in the form of acts. Applications of trips and outings, and application of participation in physical labour is needed in actual life for following various professions.

22

HOME: THE MOULDING CENTRE

Under the stress and strain of economic conditions and with the growth of industrialisation, the institution of home has broken down. The parents and guardians have little time and energy to look after their wards. Much cannot be expected out of them. Yet, they may maintain a peaceful and loving life. They may follow virtuous and religious life performing with proper decorum. Traditional rites at least in minimum degree must be taught to our children. Children should participate in those rites with full faith, devotion and a sense of duty. This will go a long way towards inculcating good conduct and discipline in them. Other individuals and neighbours must also be helpful by setting up standard of good behaviour in their own lives. Children learn by imitation the life of teachers. Wardens, parents and neighbours have their impact upon the impressionable minds of the children. They have to realize this and mould their life properly.

SPIRIT OF DISCIPLINE

The spirit of discipline is needed for national re-organisation as visualised by the Sangh. But it is not of the police or the military type. It is self-restrained discipline. Discipline nurtured in the Sangh is a self-restraint of cultured people. It is discipline where one feels that he has a higher duty to the nation and that his personal and family wants can wait. He prepares himself to respond to higher call in a well-ordered and co-ordinated manner. It is the type of discipline where all will put together their intelligence, feelings, physical energies and their material possessions in the great cause of national welfare.

This spirit of willing self-restraint and self-sacrifice makes out a person who undergoes training in the Shakha. He is called a "Swayamsevak". A Swayamsevak is not a mere volunteer- as is ordinarily understood these days- who move about in uniform in certain public occasions and participate in the physical demonstration. No. He is not a passive entity simply carrying out some manual workforce of change at the bidding of others. A Swayamsevak has a mission with a national vision.

23

BHAGWA DHWAJ AND CALL TO THE GURU

Bhagwa Dhwaj is the greatest national symbol. It signifies sacrifice, knowledge, renunciation and service. Sri Guru Poornima which is also called Vyasa Poornima is an occasion of great significance and sanctity for us. It was the great sage—Vyasa who classified and organised the vast storehouse of knowledge—the Vedas. He highlighted the sublime virtues and values of life evolved in Bharat Varsha over the ages and offered a beautiful synthesis of the thought and practice embedded therein. His work stands as a lighthouse of guidance not only for our countrymen but for the entire humanity. Ved Vyasa, therefore, is rightly called Jagad Guru and world preceptor. It is because of this that Guru Pooja is also known as Vyasa Pooja.

On this day, we offer our worship to our Guru, whoever he may be, and place at his feet our humble offering. We seek his blessings and resolve to march ahead on the path of our ideal life in the light of his guidance.

So far as set up of our organisation is concerned, we have not looked down upon any particular individual as the Guru scriptures have eulogised in glowing terms the qualities of the Guru and placed him on a pedestal equal to God Himself. Naturally, it would be impossible to find such a Guru in every person. No mortal can ever be expected to be perfect without any blemish or shortcoming. And, after all, a human being is a fleeting entity. He cannot be a permanent guide for a nation from generation to generation.

We, in Sangh, have chosen a symbol which would at once reflect the highest and noblest of our national heritage. And that is the Bhagwa Dhwaj.

YAJNA SYMBOLISES

Yajna sacrifice occupies a pivotal position in our cultural heritage. The term Yajna carries meaning of offering one's individual life in the cause of social regeneration to Yajna. We offer an oblation all that is unworthy, undesirable and unholy in us in the fire of virtues. In Yajna, we take to a fiery path of dedication. Sacrifice, service and penance are the very essence of Yajna. The presiding deity of Yajna is fire. Flame represents the fire and the sacred Bhagwa Dhwaj is the symbol of the orange coloured sacrificial flames.

FLAG OF BHAGWAN

We are the devotees of Shraddha, faith and not of superstition. We are the devotees of knowledge and not of ignorance. Our seers did severe penance to get rid of ignorance and to attain the light of truth and everlasting knowledge. Darkness represents ignorance and the sun represents the light of knowledge. In our ancient literature, the sun—Suryanarayana is described as sitting in a chariot drawn by seven horses. And before He arrives on the sky, the saffron-colour flag fluttering from his chariot appears on the eastern horizon in shining colours. It is symbolic of the sunrise dispelling darkness and heralding the coming of day light. That flag of Bhagwan Suryanarayana is the flag of Bhagwan—God Himself that later on became Bhagwa Dhwaj. The highest stage of the human development is represented by the fourth and the final *ashrama*—the *sannyasa*—which demands a spirit of total renunciation and service. The *sannyasi* has to tread unflinchingly on the fiery path of self-sacrifice. As a constant reminder of his sacrificial life, the *sannyasi* wears the Bhagwa Dhwaj. Thus, Bhagwa has been the symbol of the highest principle and practice evolved over ages in this sacred land. Now, what is our attitude of worshipping such a Guru? The true importance of worship lies in trying to assimilate in our life the qualities symbolised by the Guru. Thus, to become more and more identical with the Guru himself would be the real worship.

The earning that we make on this day of Guru Pooja in the form of money is to remind ourselves that the earning that we make all our life is made possible because of the co-operation of society. Not only the financial earnings but our entire happiness is a thing which has been given by society. And as such, it becomes our duty to pay back that social debt to the maximum extent possible for us. In fact, the daily one-hour Shakha wherein we offer our body, mind and intellect is intended to fulfil the social obligation in our daily life. It is in tune with this spirit of self-offering in Sangh that the system of *Guru Dakshina* has also been evolved.

24

BUILDING UNSHAKABLE COMRADESHIP

In the case of our brethren in society, the question of their inborn hostility does not arise. A worker is often born out of ignorance. He is bound to be short-lived. So, he should approach every individual, whatever be his present aptitude and position in life, in a spirit of friendliness and equality and with faith in his innate goodness. He must be confident of triumphing over the various weaknesses, vices and temperamental differences of others on the strength of his genuine love and regard for them and the example of his own sterling character.

Good character alone is not enough. There are persons endowed with pure character but who are rude and offensive in their speech and behaviour. They even pride themselves on their rudeness. They say, "I call a spade a spade. If it offends anyone, I cannot let him go harmlessly". But a worker who is dedicated to national re-organisation cannot afford to be so. Sweetness of speech is a must for a national worker.

BE SELF-CONFIDENT

Beware of self-conceit. All our great men have invariably commanded everyone. It does not, however, mean that a worker should lose his self-confidence while moving with men or facing difficult situations. Self-confidence is, in fact, in very life breath of all great workers.

It is the calm and concerted efforts and self-confidence that can move mountains. The tranquillity of mind born out of supreme confidence is power. Anger and excitement ruin the power of calm judgement and firm action. However, a worker should not become a victim of self-conceit in the name of self-confidence, nor should he lose self-confidence in an attempt to become unassuming and humble. The correct poise of mind should be cultivated assiduously.

25

ONE LIFE ONE MISSION

Through introspection, the worker should be able to discern correctly to what extent he has progressed in identifying himself with the mission of building an organised national life. Whether the mission has become his all consuming passion, moving and swaying his thoughts, feelings and actions in company or in solitude. The character of a person lies in what he thinks and what he does when he is alone. Character matters much especially today when young minds are surrounded by innumerable temptations of modern civilization like vulgar pictures, songs, films, novels and entertainments.

DAILY SELF CORRECTION

To do this, it is necessary for the worker to sit on solitude daily in the morning and at night and prose his mind. With a discerning intellect, he must find out whether any evil thought entered his mind. If so, he should resolve to throw it out and become purer from the next day. He should detach his mind from unruly associations and make it immersed in thoughts concerned with the chosen mission of his life. It is possible that he succumbs to the same feelings on the next day also. But he need not despair. He should continue his drive for self-searching. He will, in course of time, become less prone to evil propensities and more attuned to the noble impulses.

The daily recitation of our *prarthana* is a powerful act in this process. One should be particular not only in the correct pronunciation of each and every word and syllable, but also about the thought-content of every word. Such repeated impressions will, in course of time, shape one's character accordingly.

THE JOY OF SELF-SURRENDER

The spring of spontaneous joy and inspiration that rises in one's heart changes with a spirit of total surrender to that ideal. This will defeat all forces of darkness and despair. No great work is achieved without great suffering and sacrifice. The worker will be required to pay a heavy price in terms of his personal and family happiness and similarly embrace life of the troubles or dangers in treading the path of the ideal. The glowing examples of Sri Rama is there as the guiding star for the hazardous voyage of life.

26

RSS AND SOCIETAL REFORMS
PARTICIPATION IN LAND REFORMS

The RSS volunteers participated in the Bhoodan movement organised by the Gandhian leader Vinoba Bhave. Well, Vinoba Bhave had met RSS leader M. S. Golwalkar in Meerut in November 1951. Golwalkar had been inspired by the movement that encouraged land reforms through voluntary people. He praised the support of the RSS for this movement. Consequently, many RSS volunteers led by Nanaji Deshmukh participated in the movement. But Golwalkar was also critical of the Bhoodan movement on other occasions for being reactionary and for working merely with a view to counteracting communalism. He believed that the movement should inculcate a faith in the masses that would make them rise above the base of communalism.

REFORM IN CASTES

The RSS has advocated the training for Dalits and other backward classes as temple high priests (a position traditionally reserved for the caste Brahmins and denied to the lower castes). They urge that the social divisiveness of the caste system is responsible for the lack of adherence to Hindu values and traditions and that reaching out to the lower castes in this manner will be a remedy to the problem. The RSS has also condemned upper caste Hindus for preventing Dalits from worshipping at temple saying that even God will desert the temple in which Dalits enter.

RELIEF AND REHABILITATION

The RSS was instrumental in relief efforts in 1971 Orissa cyclone, in 1977 Andhra Pradesh cyclone and in 1984 Bhopal gas disaster. It assisted in relief efforts during the 2001 Gujarat earthquakes and helped rebuild villages. Approximately 35,000 RSS members in uniform were engaged in the relief efforts in Gujarat and many of the critics acknowledged their vital role. An RSS affiliated NGO, Seva Bharati, conducted relief operations in the aftermath of the 2004 Indian Ocean earthquake.

Activities included building shelter for the victims and providing food, clothes and medical necessities. The RSS assisted relief efforts during the Sumatra earthquakes and tsunami in 2004 and in subsequent years. Seva Bharati also adopted 57 children (28 Muslims and 19 Hindus) from military affected areas of Jammu and Kashmir. It provided them education up to higher secondary level. It also took care of the victims of the KARGIL WAR.

In 2006, RSS participated in relief efforts to provide basic necessities such as food, milk and potable water to the people of Surat, Gujarat who were affected by floods in the region. The RSS volunteers carried out relief and rehabilitation work after the floods affected North Karnataka and some districts of the State of Andhra Pradesh. In 2013, following the Uttarakhand floods, RSS volunteers were involved in flood relief work through its offices set up at affected areas.

RECEPTION

Sardar Vallabhabhai Patel, the first Deputy Prime Minister and Home Minister of India, said in January, 1948 that the RSS activists were patriots who love their country. He asked the RSS to join the Congress knowing that the members of the RSS are the defenders of the Hinduism.

Field marshal K. M. Kariappa in his speech to RSS volunteers said: "RSS is in one's heart. My dear young men! Do not be disturbed by uncharitable comments of uninterested person. Look ahead! Go ahead! The country is standing in need of your services."

Zakir Hussain, the former President of India told in Milad Mehfil in Monghyar on 20 November, 1949: "The allegations against the RSS of violence and hatred against Muslims are wholly false. Muslims should learn the lesson of mutual love and cooperation from the RSS."

A Gandhian leader and the leader of Sarvodaya Movement, Jay Prakash Narayan, had the following to say in 1977: "RSS is a revolutionary organisation. No other organisation in the country comes anywhere near it. It alone has the capacity to transform society and wipe the tears from the eyes of the poor." He further added: "I have great expectation from this revolutionary organisation which has taken up the challenges of creating a new India."

27

ACHIEVEMENT OF RSS

The biggest achievement of the RSS is that it has been successful in protecting the nascent flame of nationalism and patriotism for the past 94 years. With the educational institutions unfiltered and suffered with leftist-ideology and the great history of the country to suit a new ideologies, it is really a surprise that the force came to the core and they could help form a government. Given that the followers of Sanatana Dharma are divided for the past 1000 + years riddled with all sorts of division on grounds of caste, creed, language, religion, sex, education etc. It was almost an impossible task to stick together a harmonic fabric of the society. All this has ensured that we as a people remain self-flagging; depressed with self-respect leaving aside anything to be proud of. This has been reined in by RSS with its limited resources and Spartan life style and with the sacrifices of the innumerable people who silently gave away their lives.

The RSS has inspired several organisations. It has full time driven its activities to the present. During partition, the then Prime Minister Pt. Jawaharlal Nehru was fighting to stop the bloodshed due to communal riots, it was RSS to set up thousands of relief camps to help the people migrating from the present Pakistan. The RSS played a critical part in liberation of Goa, Dadra and Nagar Haweli from Portuguese Central to become Union Territories of India.

They also played important role in Bangladesh liberation. They were the first group to donate blood for the injured army personnel. They were the first group to volunteer and help the victims of a various natural and man-made disasters like Kargil War 1999, Bhopal gas tragedy 1984, earthquake in Gujarat in 2004 and Uttarakhand floods in 2013 for the injured army personnel. Thus, we can say proudly that the RSS has played a pivotal role in the making of India and welfare of the Indians.